Why Is This Festival Special?

Hanukkah

Jillian Powell

A⁺
Smart Apple Media

First published in 2005 by Franklin Watts
96 Leonard Street, London EC2A 4XD

Franklin Watts Australia
Level 17/207 Kent Street, Sydney NSW 2000

Series editor: Sarah Peutrill, Art director: Jonathan Hair, Designer: Ian Thompson,
Picture researcher: Diana Morris, Consultant: Jonathan Gorsky, Council of
Christians and Jews

Picture credits: Brand X/Superstock: front cover t, 14. I. Genut/ArkReligion:
12, 13t, 26. Arnold Gold/New Haven Register/Image Works/Topham: 11b.
John Griffin/Image Works/Topham: 3,7. Monika Graff/Image Works/Topham:
17t. Hanan Isachar/ArkReligion: 23b. Hanan Isachar/Israel Images: 22, 23t.
Larry Kolvoord/Image Works/Topham: 10t. David Lassman/Image Works/Topham:
13b. Gideon Mendel/Corbis: 25. Ray Moller: 10b, 15, 20, 21. Richard T.
Nowitz/Corbis: 24. Picturepoint/Topham: 6br. Sybil Shapiro/ArkReligion: 18.
Shaffer Smith/Superstock: 19t. Liba Taylor/Hutchison: 6cl, 27. Topham: 8, 9.

Published in the United States by Smart Apple Media
2140 Howard Drive West, North Mankato, Minnesota 56003

Library of Congress Cataloging-in-Publication Data

Powell, Jillian.
Hanukkah / by Jillian Powell.
p. cm. — (Why is this festival special?)
Reprint. Originally published: London : Franklin Watts, 2005.
Includes index.
ISBN-13 : 978-1-58340-944-2
1. Hanukkah—Juvenile literature. I. Title.

BM695.H3P69 2006
296.4'35—dc22   2005052556

9 8 7 6 5 4 3 2 1

Contents

A festival of lights

Hanukkah is the Jewish festival of lights.

It celebrates light in the short days of November or December. The festival begins on the 25th day of the Jewish month of Kislev (see page 29) and lasts for eight days.

A Jewish boy wearing a skull cap called a kippah reads from the Torah (also shown below).

Jews follow a religion called Judaism. They try to follow the rules and laws written in their holy book, the Torah. They believe that God taught them these laws through the prophet Moses.

At Hanukkah, Jews remember a time when the Jewish people fought to be free to follow their religion. The lights of Hanukkah stand for the freedom to follow their religion and beliefs.

66 Hanukkah is sometimes close to Christmastime. We have twinkle lights and decorations, and we give presents like people do at Christmas. 99

Rebecca, age 9

Hanukkah is a time for Jewish families to be together at home.

The Hanukkah story

At Hanukkah, Jews celebrate a miracle that saved the Holy Temple of Jerusalem.

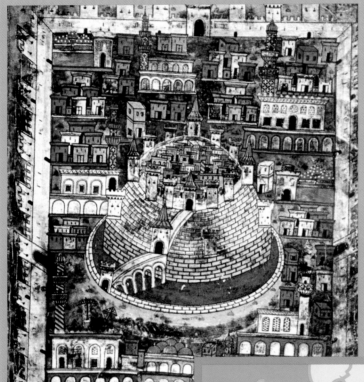

They remember a time more than 2,000 years ago when the Syrian-Greeks ruled in Judea, which is part of modern-day Israel.

The King of the Syrian-Greeks, Antiochus IV, attacked the Holy Temple in Jerusalem and stopped Jews from worshiping there.

An old picture of the walled city of Jerusalem.

Israel is in a region called the Middle East in Asia.

EUROPE

MIDDLE EAST

Israel

AFRICA

But in 164 B.C., in a town called Modin, the Jews began to fight back. They freed Jerusalem and the Holy Temple and began to clean and prepare it so that Jews could worship there again.

It was important to light the golden menorah (a kind of lamp) in the Temple, but there was only enough oil to last one day. The Jews knew it would take eight days to get more. But the oil kept the lamp burning for eight days.

This is the miracle that Jews celebrate at Hanukkah.

"We did a play at school about finding the oil in the Temple, and how it kept burning so Jews could worship again."

Daniel, age 10

The menorah

Jews remember the miracle in the Temple by lighting candles.

Jewish school-children light candles in a menorah in their classroom.

Each day, in homes and synagogues, Jews light one candle in a menorah. This is a candlestick that can hold nine candles. They use one candle to light one more candle each day after sunset until all of the candles are lit at the end of the festival.

The menorah has nine candle holders. There are eight candles, one for each night of Hanukkah. The ninth candle, called the Shammes, is used to light the others.

The menorah is put by a window or door so that everyone can see the lights burning. The lights must not be used for anything except to remind people of the Hanukkah miracle. Sometimes, everyone in a family has his or her own menorah.

❝ *My sister and I each have our own menorah. It's a special part of the day when we light the candles.* **❞**

Naomi, age 10

Menorahs come in many different sizes and can be beautifully decorated.

When the candles are lit, families spend time teaching children about Hanukkah or enjoying songs and games together.

A giant menorah in a park in Connecticut.

11

Prayers, songs, and blessings

Hanukkah is celebrated with many prayers, songs, and blessings.

There are services in synagogues every morning of the festival. There are readings from the Torah, songs, and prayers, including a special prayer for Hanukkah called "Al Hanissim."

> " *I was asked to light the candles in the menorah in our synagogue last year.* "
> Nathan, age 10

These boys are praying in their synagogue.

After prayers, everyone sings the group of psalms called the Hallel. This is when the candles in the menorah are lit, often by children.

At home, Jews sing blessings and prayers as they light the candles in the menorah. They sing three blessings on the first night, and two on the other nights of the festival.

Children singing psalms at a Hanukkah service. They each wear a prayer shawl (tallis).

Children also sing songs about Hanukkah at school.

Children sing about the number of candles on a menorah.

13

Games

Families like to have fun and play games together at Hanukkah.

The dreidel game is a popular game of chance. A dreidel is a spinning top that has a Hebrew letter on each of its four sides.

Each player takes a turn spinning the dreidel.

There is a story that says the dreidel game began when Jews were kept from reading their holy book, the Torah, by the Syrian-Greeks. Jewish people got together to secretly study the Torah, but whenever a Syrian-Greek soldier went past, they took out their dreidels and pretended to play with them.

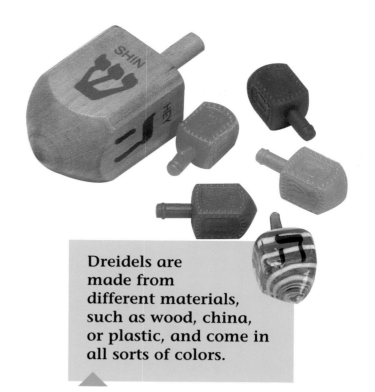

Dreidels are made from different materials, such as wood, china, or plastic, and come in all sorts of colors.

Children may also play board games or do special craft projects or puzzles at Hanukkah. Games and puzzles are often decorated with Hanukkah candles and dreidels.

Pictures made with sand and a children's puzzle decorated with the symbols of Hanukkah.

Cards and gifts

Jewish families exchange cards and gifts to wish each other "Happy Hanukkah."

Sometimes, children make their own Hanukkah cards at home or in school. They may decorate them with menorahs or dreidels.

HAPPY HANUKKAH

Hanukkah cards made from colored paper and decorated with a menorah and dreidel.

Happy Hanukkah

Children may be given presents in grab bags. These contain surprise gifts such as candy and small toys or games. Hanukkah gifts are always small because this is a religious festival and not just about food or presents.

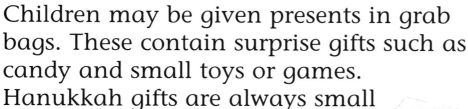

Colorful menorahs designed as gifts for children.

Some families like to give small gifts on each of the eight nights of the festival. It is traditional for parents and grandparents to give children yellow bags of real or chocolate money. This is called gelt.

Children may receive chocolate coins wrapped in gold paper.

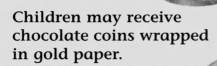

17

Decorations

Decorations are important at Hanukkah.

In Israel and in Jewish communities around the world, people put up decorations outside.

> **"** *I like helping to put up the decorations for Hanukkah. Dad puts twinkle lights at the front of the house.* **"**
> Nathan, age 10

A giant menorah and twinkle lights decorate a street in Israel.

Many Jewish families decorate inside their homes for the festival, too. They put out menorahs and sometimes hang twinkle lights.

Jews also hang banners and paper decorations showing menorahs, candles, dreidels, and the Star of David.

Decorative dreidels hanging in a Jewish home.

The six-pointed Star of David is a Jewish symbol throughout the world.

The traditional colors for Hanukkah are blue and white, the color of the sky or heavens. This reminds people that the miracle of Hanukkah comes from God.

19

Festive food

Many foods eaten at Hanukkah are fried in oil to remind people of the miracle of the Temple lamp.

In Israel and parts of the Middle East, north Africa, and southern Europe, Jewish families eat fried doughnuts called *sufganiya*.

The doughnuts have jam inside.

Cheese and other dairy foods are eaten in many Hanukkah dishes.

Cheese is another traditional food for Hanukkah. It reminds Jews of the story of Judith, who helped the Jews fight against the Syrian-Greeks. She fed the Syrian-Greek general salty cheese. This made him so thirsty that he drank a lot of wine and became drunk, so Judith was able to cut off his head!

Jews from eastern Europe cook latkes, which are pancakes made with eggs and potatoes. They eat them with onions and vegetables or as a dessert, with honey and spices.

This tradition has spread to other parts of the world, such as America.

" I help mom make cookies at Hanukkah. We make them in Hanukkah shapes like dreidels and menorahs. "

Jess, age 9

Hanukkah holiday

In Israel, everyone gets free time for Hanukkah.

There are many special events in which people get together to light menorahs or go to dinners, parties, and concerts. Some towns and cities have a fun fair for the children and a craft fair with festive foods and presents on sale.

> **"** *I look forward to Hanukkah because we get a whole week off school!* **"**
>
> *Alex, age 10*

A colorful street procession in Israel. This is part of the Three Holidays Festival, which celebrates Christmas, Hanukkah, and Ramadan.

Schools close for a whole week so children can celebrate the festival. Sometimes children put on plays for parents and friends.

Schoolchildren hold candles as they act out the story of Hanukkah.

Important buildings, such as the Israeli Parliament House, are decorated with giant menorahs formed by electric lights.

The City Hall in Tel Aviv, Israel, lit up as a giant menorah.

Torch relay

Hanukkah is celebrated each year with torch relays.

On the eve of Hanukkah, marathon runners go to the town of Modin in Israel. They light torches and then carry them all the way to the Western Wall in Jerusalem. This is the last wall left standing from the Holy Temple of Jerusalem.

A runner brings a torch to the holy site of the Western Wall in Jerusalem as the evening light fades.

Nine flames burn in the menorah at the Western Wall.

The last runner hands his torch to the chief rabbi, who lights the first candle of a giant menorah.

Young Jewish people also take part in torch relays in the United States and other countries. They carry torches to celebrate Hanukkah and to bring together Jews living in different parts of the world.

❝ Last year, we had a torch relay in our city. There was quite a crowd watching the runners who had come over from Israel to celebrate Hanukkah with us. ❞

Michael, age 10

25

Sharing and giving

Hanukkah is a time for giving to charity and thinking of others.

Many Jewish families like to give to charity at Hanukkah. This is called *tzedakah*. Children join in, sometimes giving a toy or some of their allowance money.

A Jewish child puts money into a charity box.

Family is very important to Jews. Hanukkah is a time to remember families in need.

When the menorah is lit, many families sit down together. They think about the miracle of Hanukkah and what it means to them.

The festival is a time for giving thanks to God for helping the Jews. It is also a time for helping others and thinking about those who are poor, sick, or in need.

> **"** Mom and Dad put an extra present in our Hanukkah grab bags for us to give to help children in need. **"**
>
> Rebecca, age 8

Glossary

dreidel a spinning top that can be filled with candy or money.

grab bags party bags containing surprise gifts and candy.

Hebrew the language of the Jewish people. It is the main language spoken in Israel.

latkes potato pancakes that are fried in oil.

menorah a candlestick that holds nine candles lit for Hanukkah.

miracle an amazing event that people believe God made happen.

Moses one of the first leaders of the Jews. He led them out of Egypt, where they were slaves, to be a free people.

prophet a teacher who tells people how God wants them to live.

rabbi a Jewish religious teacher.

Shammes the candle used to light the other eight candles in a menorah.

Star of David a star with six points that is used as a Jewish symbol.

synagogue a building where Jews go to worship and study.

Torah the most important Jewish holy book.

torch relay when a torch is carried and passed from one runner to another.

tzedakah money given by Jews to help the poor.

Judaism

Judaism is one of the oldest religions in the world. There are about 12 million Jews around the world, mostly living in Israel, a Jewish state, or in the U.S. Some people are Jewish but do not actively practice Judaism.

Religious Jews believe there is one God, who created everything in the universe. They believe that God chose the Jews as His people. He taught them His rules and laws through the prophet Moses. He gave them these rules to obey, and in return, He promised to look after them.

Jews worship God with ceremonies, prayers, and blessings, and by reading their holy books, especially the Torah.

Home and family life are very important to Jews. They celebrate several religious festivals each year that remember important times in their history.

Passover recalls the time when the Jews escaped from captivity in Egypt.

Shabuoth reminds Jews of the time when Moses received God's laws on Mount Sinai.

Sukkoth recalls the time that the Jews spent in the desert on their way to the Promised Land.

All of these festivals take their dates each year from the Jewish calendar, which is based on the sun and the moon. The Jewish month of Kislev, in which Hanukkah takes place, is in November or December on a Western calendar.

Index